England

by Michael Dahl

Consultant:
Julie A. Taddeo, PhD
Assistant Director, Center for British Studies
University of California, Berkeley

Capstone
press

Mankato, Minnesota

Fact Finders is published by Capstone Press
151 Good Counsel Drive, P.O. Box 669, Mankato, Minnesota 56002
www.capstonepress.com

Library of Congress Cataloging-in-Publication Data
Dahl, Michael.
    England / by Michael Dahl.
    p. cm.—(Fact finders: Questions and answers: Countries)
    Includes bibliographical references (p. 31) and index.
    ISBN 0-7368-2477-4 (hardcover)
    1. England—Juvenile literature. [1. England.] I. Title. II. Series.
DA27.5.D34 2005
942—dc22
                                                                                     2003026019

Summary: A brief introduction to England, following a simple question-and-answer
    format that discusses land features, government, housing, transportation, industries,
    education, sports, art forms, holidays, food, and family life. Includes a map, fast facts,
    and charts.

Editorial Credits
Erika L. Shores, editor; Kia Adams, series designer; Jennifer Bergstrom, book designer;
    maps.com, map illustrator; Wanda Winch, photo researcher; Scott Thoms, photo editor;
    Eric Kudalis, product planning editor

Photo Credits
Alamy/Sally Greenhill, 23; Bruce Coleman Inc./Eric G. Carle, 19; Bruce Leighty,
12–13; Corbis/Bettmann, 7; Corbis/Jennie Woodcock/Reflections Photolibrary, 16–17;
Corbis/Robbie Jack, 21; Corbis/Royalty-Free, cover (background), 4; Corel, 1;
Discology, 24–25; Getty Images Inc./UK Press, 8–9; Houserstock/Dave G. Houser, 11;
Houserstock/Ellen Barone, 15; Houserstock/Jan Butchofsky-Houser, 27; Index Stock
Imagery/Bill Bachmann, cover (foreground); Michelle Schaffer, 29 (top); Stockhaus
Limited, 29 (bottom); TRIP/B. Turner, 8

Artistic Effects
Photodisc/PhotoLink/F. Schussler, 18; Photodisc/C Squared Studios, 24 (both)

1 2 3 4 5 6 09 08 07 06 05 04

Table of Contents

Features

Where is England?

England is an island country west of Europe. England is slightly smaller than the U.S. state of Alabama.

England's landforms include rolling hills, lakes, and rivers. The Pennine Chain is a row of hills in central England. Northwest of the Pennines is England's rainy Lake District.

The Pennine Chain runs through the center of England. ▶

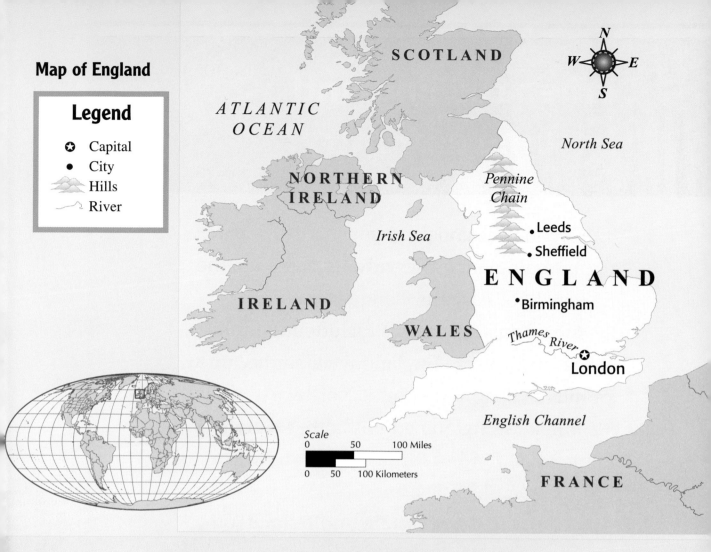

Map of England

Legend

⊗ Capital
• City
⛰ Hills
〰 River

SCOTLAND

ATLANTIC OCEAN

North Sea

NORTHERN IRELAND

Pennine Chain

• Leeds
• Sheffield

Irish Sea

E N G L A N D

IRELAND

• Birmingham

WALES

Thames River

⊗ London

English Channel

Scale

0   50   100 Miles

0   50   100 Kilometers

FRANCE

The Thames River flows through the area called the English Lowlands. It is the longest river in England. Hills and grasslands are south of the Thames. High cliffs line the southern coast of England.

When did England become a country?

England became a country in 1072. Before 1072, small, warring kingdoms made up England. William the Conqueror entered the area from France in 1066. He united the kingdoms to form England. William became known as King William I.

England later joined with other countries. England and Wales formed a **union** in 1536. In 1707, England, Wales, and Scotland became Great Britain. Great Britain and Ireland joined to become the United Kingdom in 1801.

Fact!

William I was the first king of England. Since 1952, Queen Elizabeth II has been the queen of the United Kingdom.

William the Conqueror united England in 1072.

In 1921, some counties in Ireland left the union. Six Irish counties stayed part of the United Kingdom. These counties became Northern Ireland. In 1927, the name for the union changed again. It became the United Kingdom of Great Britain and Northern Ireland.

What type of government does England have?

The United Kingdom's government is called a **constitutional monarchy**. England and the other countries in the United Kingdom follow the same laws.

Parliament makes laws and runs the United Kingdom. A **prime minister** is a member of Parliament and the head of government. Parliament meets in the Palace of Westminster in England's capital, London.

The Palace of Westminster is home to Big Ben. The clocktower is a famous site in London. ▶

Queen Elizabeth II attends parades and other events in England.

Near the Palace of Westminster sits Buckingham Palace. This palace is the official home of the ruling **monarch**. The king or queen represents England and the United Kingdom at events.

What kind of housing does England have?

Most people in England live in modern houses or apartment buildings. People call apartments flats. People who live in flats may use elevators to travel between floors. Elevators are called lifts in England.

Where do people in England live?

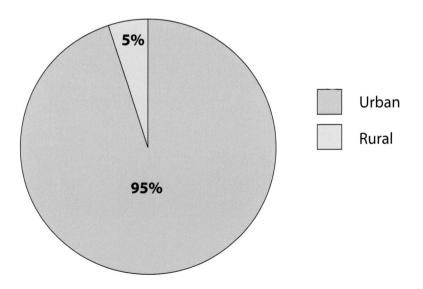

5%

95%

Urban
Rural

Some English homes in the country have thatched roofs.

About five percent of people in England live on farms or in small villages. Some country homes have thatched roofs. The tightly packed straw, hay, or grass keeps out rain.

What are England's forms of transportation?

England has most forms of transportation. Cars, bicycles, and motorcycles move along city streets. Red double-decker buses are a common sight in London. Airplanes take off and land at airports around the country.

London has the oldest underground railway system in the world. Electric trains carry people through tunnels built beneath the city.

Fact!

The Chunnel is a railway tunnel that runs below the English Channel. High-speed trains travel through the Chunnel between England and France.

Many people travel through London's busy streets on buses.

Londoners call the railway the Tube. The Tube brings people to train stations in London. Trains leave every hour for places throughout the United Kingdom.

What are England's major industries?

Many people work in England's service industry. They work as teachers, bankers, or salespeople. Tourism is another part of England's service industry. Each year, millions of people visit Buckingham Palace, museums, and churches in England.

England also has many factories. Some companies make materials for medicines and paints. Other companies make clothes. Some factories make electronic equipment and engines for airplanes.

What does England import and export?

Imports	Exports
manufactured goods	food and beverages
food products	manufactured goods
	chemicals

Visitors to London watch parades in front of Buckingham Palace.

Many **natural resources** are found in England. Coal, oil, and gas are used to make electricity. Wheat is the largest crop in England. Farmers also grow **barley**, peas, beans, and other vegetables.

What is school like in England?

Free public education is open to all children in England. Children between age 5 and 16 must attend school. The school year lasts from September to July.

Most students wear uniforms to school. Boys wear black or gray pants or shorts. Girls might wear black or gray skirts. Both boys and girls wear a white shirt and a blazer. A blazer is a jacket or sweater with a school **emblem** on it.

Fact!

Some students in England continue their education at universities. England's Oxford University and Cambridge University are two of the oldest universities in the world.

Students in England go to school Monday through Friday.

Some families pay for their children to go to private schools. Students at private schools usually live in housing at the school. The students go home on weekends and holidays.

What are England's favorite sports and games?

Cricket is the national sport of England. Cricket teams play on a field called a green. In cricket, a batter receives balls from the bowler, or pitcher. The batter tries to keep a thrown ball from knocking over three wooden stakes in the ground behind him. The batter may also try to hit the ball to score a run.

Fact!

England has hosted the Lawn Tennis Championships at Wimbledon since 1877. Each year, pro tennis players from around the world compete on the grass courts at Wimbledon.

Cricket is played on greens in England.

Some people think of soccer as England's national sport. In England, soccer is called football. English football teams are famous around the world.

What are the traditional art forms in England?

England is known for its literature and theater art forms. Many world-famous writers were born in England. Beatrix Potter and A. A. Milne wrote many stories for children. Many people think William Shakespeare was the greatest English writer to ever live. Today, about 1,500 movies have been made from his plays.

Fact!

The Mousetrap *is a murder mystery play by English writer Agatha Christie.* The Mousetrap *is the world's longest running play. Since 1952, the play has been performed at least 20,000 times in London.*

Theaters in England often perform Hamlet *and other plays written by William Shakespeare.*

People enjoy going to plays in England. England's Royal Shakespeare Theatre puts on many of Shakespeare's plays each year. Modern plays and musicals are performed at theaters in London and other cities across England.

What major holidays do people in England celebrate?

People in England celebrate Boxing Day on December 26. Long ago, rich people gave their workers the day after Christmas off. Servants received wrapped gifts in boxes. Some people think that is how the holiday got its name. Today, English people take the day off from work. They give presents to their friends.

What other holidays do people in England celebrate?

Christmas Day
Good Friday
Easter Sunday
Remembrance Day (Poppy Day)

On Guy Fawkes Day, some children make dummies to burn in bonfires.

Guy Fawkes Day is on November 5. In 1605, Guy Fawkes led a plan to blow up Parliament. His plan failed. Modern celebrations remember the night the plot was stopped. People go to bonfires and watch fireworks on Guy Fawkes Day.

What are the traditional foods of England?

Typical English meals include meat served with potatoes or other vegetables. Favorite dinner dishes are roast beef, Yorkshire pudding, and shepherd's pie. Yorkshire pudding is a batter cooked in meat fats. Shepherd's pie is made of ground beef and mashed potatoes.

Fact!

Cabbage, brussels sprouts, lettuce, peas, and carrots are often served with English dishes. Farmers can grow these vegetables in England's mild weather.

Fish and chips are served wrapped in paper.

In the afternoon, the English enjoy tea. Tea is served with cookies called biscuits.

Fish and chips is a famous English dish. To make fish and chips, whitefish is dipped in golden batter and fried. Salt and vinegar are added to potato fries, called chips.

What is family life like in England?

Like families in other modern countries, English mothers and fathers usually both work. Children go to school. After school, students study and spend time with friends. Children also go to concerts or movies. On weekends, many families enjoy hiking outdoors or playing sports and games.

What are the ethnic backgrounds of people in England?

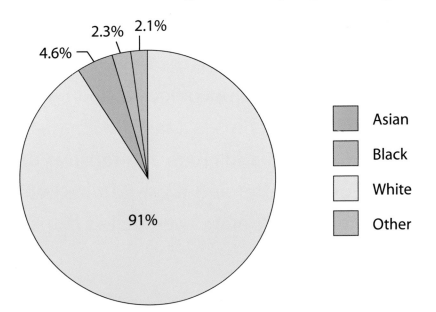

On weekends, English families spend time together at parks.

England has become a country of **immigrants**. People from India, Pakistan, Somalia, and China have moved to England. These families celebrate the food, clothing, and music of their homelands. But they all think of themselves as English.

England Fast Facts

Official name:

England, part of the United Kingdom of Great Britain and Northern Ireland

Land area:

50,333 square miles (130,362 square kilometers)

Average annual precipitation:

33 inches (84 centimeters)

Average January temperature:

38 degrees Fahrenheit (3 degrees Celsius)

Average July temperature:

60 degrees Fahrenheit (15.5 degrees Celsius)

Population:

49,138,831 people

Capital city:

London

Language:

English

Natural resources:

coal, natural gas, petroleum

Religions:

Christian	*71.6%*
Other	*23.6%*
Islamic	*2.7%*
Hindu	*1%*
Sikh	*0.69%*
Jewish	*0.5%*

Money and Flag

Money:

England's money is the pound sterling. One pound equals 100 pence. In 2004, 1 U.S. dollar equaled 0.57 pound. One Canadian dollar equaled 0.42 pound.

Flag:

England does not have an official flag. The flag called the St. George's Cross has been used for centuries. This flag has a white background and a red cross. The United Kingdom's flag is the Union Jack. It is red, white, and blue. It has a red cross through the center.

Learn to Speak British English

People in England often use different words for everyday things than people in the United States do. Below are some words used in England.

American	British
french fries	chips
hood of a car	bonnet
police officer	bobby
sweater	jumper
thank you, goodbye	cheers
toilet	loo
truck	lorry
trunk of a car	boot

Glossary

barley (BAR-lee)—a common type of grain; grains are the seeds of a cereal plant.

constitutional monarchy (kon-sti-TOO-shuhn-uhl MON-ar-kee)—a system of government in which the monarch's powers are limited

emblem (EM-bluhm)—a symbol or a sign that stands for something

immigrant (IM-uh-gruhnt)—a person who comes to live permanently in a country

industry (IN-duh-stree)—a single branch of business or trade

monarch (MON-ark)—a ruler, such as a king or queen, who often inherits his or her position

natural resource (NACH-ur-uhl REE-sorss)—a material found in nature that is useful to people

Parliament (PAR-luh-muhnt)—the group of lawmakers that makes laws in the United Kingdom

prime minister (PRIME MIN-uh-stur)—the person in charge of the government in some countries

union (YOON-yuhn)—two or more things or people joined together to form a larger group

Internet Sites

FactHound offers a safe, fun way to find Internet sites related to this book. All of the sites on FactHound have been researched by our staff.

Here's how:
1. Visit *www.facthound.com*
2. Type in this special code **0736824774** for age-appropriate sites. Or enter a search word related to this book for a more general search.
3. Click on the **Fetch It** button.

FactHound will fetch the best sites for you!

Read More

Deady, Kathleen W. *England.* Countries of the World. Mankato, Minn.: Bridgestone Books, 2001.

Gray, Susan Heinrichs. *England.* First Reports. Minneapolis: Compass Point Books, 2002.

Olson, Kay Melchisedech. *England.* Many Cultures, One World. Mankato, Minn.: Blue Earth Books, 2003.

Index

DATE DUE

Demco, Inc. 38-293

J. C. BUSH SCHOOL